TIPS From Your GRANDAD

YOU CAN DO IT!

ROBYN PATERSON

PHOTOGRAPHY BY **TAMMY WILLIAMS**

PIER 9

CONTENTS

INTRODUCTION

Introduction

I had just watched a documentary (ok, it was a reality show) about a bunch of overweight Westerners who were placed with a Nepalese family in the Himalayas. The point was that, after a month of eating yak's liver and lentils, they would turn away from their collective former habit of thinking a good dinner was deep-fried bacon, tinned spaghetti and a cigarette.

It kind of worked. But what stood out to me, far more than the 'OMG she lost, like, five centimetres of hip fat!', was the sense of purpose and tangible happiness they had gained from learning they could do things for themselves. From making a fire to fixing a wheel on a cart, their self-esteem soared and the moping stopped. And the idea for this book was born.

I'm not suggesting we all go harness a yak and whip up a survival hut. But I do believe we get a deep primal satisfaction from conquering the simple things in life. I felt like a fully-fledged, lycra-clad superhero the day I changed a washer in a tap for the first time.

Many of us had grandparents or great-grandparents who did it all. We've grown up hearing endless tales beginning 'In my day …' We rolled our eyes and distracted grandad with the racing channel. But now the plug has fallen out from the belly of the Great Global Piggy Bank, and worse than that — frankly — we're bored: bored with the heels falling off the shoes we bought last week; bored with recalled, hot pink, lead-based (it turns out) toys; bored with patronising mechanics, and bored with having to pay someone to do every darned thing that needs done. 'Grandad!' we yell into his hearing aid, 'Tell me about the time you painted that wall again …'

Fear not, brothers and sisters, we're taking the power back. We all knew Nana and her shed full of jam jars had a lot to offer, but it turns out Grandad does too — and I don't just mean puns. *Tips from your Grandad* is a book to keep close at hand. Like *Tips from your Nana*, it will help you save the environment, it will help you save society, and better yet — let's face it, we're children of our time — it will help you save money.

Hidden in pockets of our world are people — men and women — who still know how to do stuff. Some of them remember the Great Depression, or a few of the not-so-great ones since. Some of them are bright young Gen-Y types who realised self-sufficiency was cool again before the rest of us did. Some of them grew up in countries where DIY is the only option. Even more of them have been brought together in this book to show you 'how to' do a great list of basic things, without complicated equipment or expensive supplies. From changing a tyre to catching a fish and smoking it in your backyard — YOU can do it!

Robyn Paterson, May 2010

Neil Lambie says: Time spent on reconnaissance is seldom wasted.

CHAPTER ONE
THE GREAT OUTDOORS

Planting trees with Des

Whether you're doing it for green points, shade, wind shelter, hiding from the neighbours, or simply to make your house look more expensive, there may come a time when you want to plant a tree. Good on you.

Des Smith can't say enough about the advantages of trees — he's passionate about them. Native trees, fruit trees, whatever trees; Des has been planting them since he was knee high to a grasshopper. If you can't plant one at home, he suggests, join a group or put one in a community plot.

Des says: Just get out there and bloody well plant one!

He proudly tells the story of a friend from New York who had never planted a tree. Des helped him plant some when on a visit, and now the friend often calls just to find out how 'his trees' are getting on. We humans have had a long connection to trees, which possibly explains why getting them started is so therapeutic. Our early ancestors used to revere them; trees pretty much sustain life on earth, and (if you go all Darwin on it) we probably lived in them once upon a time.

Planting a tree is not as intimidating as you might imagine, and you don't need to pay a landscaper half your income to do it.

1. CHOOSE YOUR TREE

Think about what your baby tree is going to grow up to be. If you're picking one for outside a window, for example, you're not going to want a towering jungle plant. Des recommends planting trees indigenous to your area — not only because it encourages their survival, but also because they'll be naturally suited to your soil type. Personally, I like plants that give back — it's fruit trees for me! Try to imagine what your tree will look like when it is established, and check whether or not it can handle your local climate.

2. CHOOSE YOUR SPOT

This is vital — don't skip this bit. It might sound simple, but it could save you a big headache later on! How your tree will look, how it will behave and what it will need are major factors to consider — a bit like a pet. Most importantly, remember that trees don't

just grow above ground — there's almost as much action below. Planting them too close to a building or above your plumbing can cause havoc later on, so pick a good spot away from trouble and you won't have to worry.

3. DRAINAGE

Most trees aren't too keen on having soggy feet, so once you've decided on a home for your tree, check that the soil has reasonable drainage. The easiest way is to dig a small hole and fill it with water. If the water's still there in a couple of hours, best pick another spot.

4. CONGRATULATIONS, IT'S A TREE

Pick up your chosen sapling from the nursery, and carry it home proudly in a plastic bag. Soak the roots in a bucket of water. You'll notice bubbles appearing as the young tree has a good drink — when these bubbles stop, it's done soaking. Take the tree out and leave it to drain.

5. GET DIGGING

While your sapling is draining it's time for the fun part; digging a hole. The best tool for the job is a good, strong, steel spade — the shaft and the spade bit should all be one piece of steel. Don't be tempted by the cheap ones, especially if your soil is hard — or you'll end up holding a stick and a piece of metal instead.

TIP: At the bottom of the hole, make the centre slightly higher than the edges. This allows the water to disperse properly.

Des says: If you don't have a spade there's no need to spend big, borrow one!

Dig a hole that is at least twice the width of the container of your young tree, but not much deeper. Too deep and the roots will suffocate, too narrow and they have no room to spread.

6. PLANTING

The time has come to introduce your tree to its new home. Place it in the hole, and surround it with some good compost (home-made of course!).

7. PATTING AND PETTING

With your hands, press the soil and compost around the base of the tree.

Des says: It doesn't need to be packed solid, Just nice and firm.

'Tickle' the top layer of dirt with your finger tips to rough it up a little so that water will get through.

8. WATERING

Give the tree a good drink of water, whether it's hot, cold, sunny or raining. Keep watering it at least once a week (more if the weather's dry) during its first month or two.

TIP: The best time to plant (depending on your climate) is usually spring or autumn. This gives the tree time to get used to the weather before it gets hit with the hard stuff.

The best time to plant a tree was 20 years ago. The next best time is now. (Chinese proverb)

Growing great fruit with Mat

Mathew Singleton can still remember the first time he ate stewed fruit. It was a sweltering hot day, and he had been hard at work on the farm next door. Lunch, supplied by the neighbour's wife, included a bowl of cold, stewed peaches, which he thought was the most refreshing thing he had ever eaten.

Inspired, Mat began to look at fruit trees in a whole new light. He planted a wealth of new varieties on his property, put renewed effort into their growth, and has eaten from their bounty every day since.

Unlike Mat, I'm not much of a gardener — I can't seem to find spare time, and I have an unfortunate tendency to forget the garden still exists during winter. But the satisfaction of eating juicy, delicious fruit from your own tree is motivation enough to give fruit-growing a go.

With a few simple tips even a beginner gardener like me can grow successful fruit. Many fruit varieties grow perfectly well in patio pots, so if you're short on space, no problem there either. Now that you're out of excuses, make like a Grandad and get to the garden centre!

TIP: Good fruit trees can be a lasting treasure. Mat still plucks pears from trees that his great-great-grandfather planted over 100 years ago.

Mat says: If you can, plant even more than two varieties of the same tree.

1. CHOOSE THE RIGHT SIZE

In Grandad's day fruit trees came in one size — large. The kind that kids climb into and transport themselves to lost lands (or just fall out of). If you have plenty of space and are keen to establish a similar heirloom, then fantastic. These days though, there is more choice. If you don't have a big garden or are opting for a pot, go for dwarf or semi-dwarf varieties.

2. CHOOSE THE RIGHT TYPE

It's tempting to get carried away at the garden centre and arrive home with glamorous-looking fruit plants from exotic locations. I have done this more than once. But learn from my mistakes, and try to choose varieties that are local to your area. They will have been bred for your climate and local soil conditions and are much more likely to survive in your garden.

3. GIVE YOUR TREE A LOVE INTEREST

Pollination is essentially plant sex, and — just as with babies — pollination needs to happen before fruit can be born. Most fruit needs some cross-pollination, where one tree is able to exchange its pollen with that of a similar tree nearby. Some trees are self-pollinating, but even they will often produce more fruit when another tree is around. Plant a buddy tree, or put your new tree near an existing one. This other tree should be the same kind of fruit (e.g. both apples), but ideally not the same variety (e.g. not both Granny Smith apples), a bit like the don't-sleep-with-your-siblings rule.

4. BRING ON THE BEES

To put it simply, pollen (which contains the male bits) needs to get to the centre of the flower (which contains the female bits). Bees carry the pollen from one to the other, and are an essential part of the fruit-growing process. Mat is alarmed at the dwindling number of bees that he has witnessed in recent years. Attracting bees to your garden or pots will have you well on your way to producing successful fruit, plus you'll be doing the environment a favour. There are many easy ways to be bee-friendly (see page 20).

Mat says: Plant things that will flower at different times of the year so there is always plenty for the bees to choose from.

5. GO ORGANIC

Mat has been growing fruit successfully for years and never uses sprays or pesticides. They are toxic, and kill the insects you want to encourage (like bees) as well as the ones you don't. Far better for the plant — and for you — to take a leaf out of Mat's book and let nature take its course. If you're having trouble with insects or fungal diseases here are a couple of easy organic recipes that are safe, cheap and effective.

Fungal problems:

Stir 2 tbsp baking soda into 1 litre of water. Pour it into a spray bottle, give it a good shake, and spray onto the plant regularly, until it's fungi-free.

Insect problems:

Mix 2 tbsp liquid soap into 1 cup of cooking oil. Top up the mixture with four litres of water, pour it all into a spray bottle, and shake it well. Spray any affected areas, shaking the bottle regularly to mix. You can also spray this mixture over the tree when it is dormant in winter, to stop insect eggs hatching come springtime.

6. PRUNE

Don't be intimidated by the idea of pruning — it's really not rocket science, usually it needs to be done only once a year, and needn't take long. In late winter or early spring, cut away any dead or diseased branches, and trim down any tired old stems to encourage new growth. Get rid of tangled or criss-crossed shoots that are getting in the way, and any branches that are broken or trying to grow towards the ground. Shape the tree as evenly as possible, and trim back any new growth from the previous season a little so the young up-and-comers don't sap all the nutrients. Most home fruit trees will function just fine with this minimal pruning, if it's done each year.

7. TIDY UP

I confess I always thought fallen fruit tree leaves were kind of quaint and pretty, but Mat tells me that leaving them on the ground can kick-start fungal diseases for your tree. Get busy with that rake and ship the leaves off to the compost bin during autumn.

TIP: Pruning a tree is akin to taking a surgeon's knife to a body, so don't just go hacking on in there. Use a sharp pair of good secateurs or a pruning saw. Always cut a branch or stem above the point where it joins onto a larger branch or stem — not right on the join or you risk damaging the tissue.

8. CATCH THE RAIN

Fruit trees need a good soak every few days when the weather is dry. Many fruit varieties prefer acidic soil, and tap water may contain lime which makes the soil less acidic after a time. If you can, collect rainwater for your fruit trees. This doesn't need to be a complex set-up to catch the run-off from your roof; it can be as simple as sticking a bucket out in a downpour. This not only helps your fruit but it also, of course, saves water and water costs.

9. FEED THE BELLY

Your tree/s will be getting ready for a big growth spurt come spring, so they'll thank you for a bit of nutrition to get them started. As spring begins, spread compost around the base of the tree as far out as the branches reach.

Don't fertilise fruit trees, apart from citrus. If you have a worm farm, vermicast (worm poo) makes an excellent natural fertiliser for your citrus. Spread the vermicast as described for compost.

Mat says: Growing fruit is all about trial and error. Don't battle too hard, the trees will let you know what they like and don't like.

10. PICK THE FRUIT!

Picking your fruit is, for most of us, the whole point of growing it in the first place. But if you're going away during fruiting season, get someone else to pick it for you (I'm sure they won't mind!) because it also helps to keep your tree healthy. The more you pick, the more energy the tree has to put into new fruit and growth. Harvesting your fruit also means the tree's branches won't be weighed down, and prevents overripe fruit from attracting pests.

Bees with benefits

It's fair to say bees can be annoying. They climb into your jam at a picnic, get stuck inside your can of drink, can't seem to grasp the concept of glass windows, and make running barefoot an adrenalin sport. But bees are an integral part of our world, and their numbers have been dropping at a scary rate over the last decade.

Bees are our friends. They provide honey, of course, and even their venom has been found to have medicinal properties. Most importantly, many plants are completely reliant on bees for pollination — they can't reproduce without them. Commercial insecticide seems to be the factor that has hit bees hardest, yet ironically it's our crops that can't do without bees. These days farmers often need to *hire* bees to pollinate their crops! That's serious stuff. The survival of some species of plants is already threatened by the lack of bees.

So the low-down is that it's time we stopped swatting bees and started attracting them — especially if you want to have any kind of garden.

The buzz

There are plenty of simple ways to make your garden (or pots) bee-friendly. Here are some basic tips:

- Give the bees a smorgasbord: plant things that will flower at different times of the year, so there's something for the bees to enjoy all year round. Even a small patch of flowering plants will do the trick.

- Native bees prefer the local diet: if you can, choose to plant some things that are native to your area.

- Pick a good planting spot: bees are well-known sunbathers and love a flower in a sunny spot. They also get tossed around by the wind, so aim for shelter.

No bees, no honey; no work, no money. (Anon)

TOP TIP: Don't use pesticides!! Even organic sprays containing pyrethrum are highly toxic to bees. Make your own bee-friendly spray (see page 18), or if you are desperately plagued by plant pests, use a pyrethrum spray at night once the bees have gone home to the hive for the evening.

TIP: Ladybirds are also great to have around, especially if you're growing fruit. Planting a patch of daisies will make your garden a ladybird's favourite hang out.

- Choose different coloured flowers: bees have a great eye for colour and aim for flowers they think will have the best pollen. Three of their favourites are blue, purple, and yellow.

- Plant in clumps: there's nothing bees like better than a whole lot of their favourite flowers all at once. Plant a pot or patch with one type of flower, then choose another for nearby.

- Stop swatting: bees are not keen on stinging you — it results in death for them so the stakes are high. Walking away usually gets rid of curious bees, as does keeping lids on outdoor food and drink. Avoid wearing perfume in the garden if you don't want them to mistake you for a flower.

Home-smoking with Ian

There couldn't be a prouder grandad than New Zealand writer Ian Wedde. His first grandchild, Sebo, is just five months old and Ian can't wait to show him the world.

Ian grew up in a small town during the 1950s, where it seemed everyone had their own vegetable garden and a stash of home-brewed beer in their garage. Naturally in those tougher times, anything produced needed to then be preserved. Nothing was wasted — any excesses were shared or exchanged with the neighbours — 'it's just what you did'.

Living near the sea meant fish was often on the menu. Ian's father and grandfather built their own cold smoker at the family bach, and regularly smoked the catch of the day. But Ian's uncle took to the rivers in waders instead, and it was his melt-in-the-mouth smoked trout that absolutely sealed Ian's love of smoked fish. 'I have to know how to do this,' he thought.

Ian proved an eager apprentice and went on to experiment with myriad different smoking techniques over the years. To this day he still smokes his own fish. It's so popular with guests that it vanishes almost as soon as it hits the table. At this stage baby grandson Sebo is still working on sitting up, but as soon as he develops fine motor skills you can bet he'll be taught the family tricks of the trade!

SMOKE YOUR OWN

Whether you've caught your own fish or picked one up from the market, you won't regret learning to smoke it. Back in the day smoking was used as a method of preserving fish and other meats, but these days the appeal is the gorgeous, distinctive, smoky flavour it creates.

Although Ian has built many different kinds of smoke houses himself, including a more complex cold smoker, he recommends buying a small portable variety, especially when first starting out. He reckons they are more cost-effective nowadays than building your own, and — although his grandfather would be horrified at the thought — they work just as well for home smoking. They are readily available from outdoor or department stores, and are small enough to be used on the barbecue or taken with you on holiday. Bonus.

This method of smoking is known as 'hot smoking'. Unlike cold smoking it is a form of cooking the food rather than preserving it so the food won't last as long, but it's quick and easy and the flavours are irresistible!

Ingredients:

1 whole fish (or other seafood)

aromatic herbs (optional)

1 portable smoker

1–2 handfuls UNTREATED sawdust (manuka, or other non-resinous wood)

honey (optional)

salt & pepper (optional)

1 splash methylated spirits (meths)

TIP: Most fish will work well in a smoker, but oily fish — like salmon, trout and mackerel — are best. Experiment to find your favourite. Ian once smoked a turbot but doesn't recommend it. It tasted alright but shrivelled in the heat and apparently came out looking like something from **Alien 2.**

1. Cut along the belly of the pre-gutted fish and prise it open so that it lies flat, its two sides flayed out.

2. Cover with a simple marinade of a little warm water combined with manuka honey and salt & pepper to taste. Ian suggests experimenting with the amounts to find your ideal flavour level. Leave the fish to marinate for about an hour.

3. Drain away the marinade, and rub the fish with a little extra salt and pepper.

4. Take the rack out of the smoker and lay the fish, skin side down, on top of it. Leave it to dry, uncovered in a cool spot away from sunlight.

5. When the surface of the fish becomes shiny and is slightly sticky to touch, it is dry enough to smoke.

TIP: Always use a smoker outdoors in the open air, never indoors. Like anything that burns, it produces the potentially dangerous gas, carbon monoxide. You're essentially creating a small fire so use common sense and keep it away from anything flammable like trees, children, or your neighbour's boat shed.

6. Scatter a handful of sawdust along the bottom of the smoker. No need to over-do it, Ian reckons a little goes a long way. If you like, you can add a handful of aromatic fresh herbs like marjoram or rosemary.

7. Fit the rack back into the smoker, with the fish still on top, and cover with the lid.

8. Put a splash of blue meths in the shallow dish provided with your smoker and set it alight (outdoors!).

9. Place the smoker over the top of the meths dish and away you go.

10. In only 10-15 minutes your fish will be about ready. Check by opening the lid and having a peek — if it looks glossy and flakes when you poke it with a fork, it's ready. You can decide how well-done you like your fish. Ian prefers to under cook rather than over cook, particularly with salmon.

Let your fish rest a while before serving it to get the most from the flavours, and allow it to cool. If you're having people over for dinner, best start the smoking in the morning if you can. Ian recommends a glass of New Zealand pinot or a sharp rosé on the side ... but, just quietly, a home-brewed beer will do nicely (page 100).

TIP: If you're in a hurry, don't stress about drying the fish. Though you'll find it in the instructions of any smoking manual, Ian has been skipping this step for years and still gets great results. If you do have time though, drying the fish helps prepare it to absorb more of the smoke - cooking it more quickly and increasing the flavour.

Build your own barbecue with Markus

Markus McIntyre was raised the son of a modern American mum, a long way away from his extended family. Not having grandparents around when growing up made the older generation seem like a huge novelty, and Markus spent as much time as possible listening to the tales of his friends' grandparents. While his mates walked away rolling their eyes as soon as Grandpa began, Markus stuck around and heard stories and tips that the others never cottoned on to.

Though his home life was far from do-it-yourself, Markus learned all kinds of tricks from the oldies of the neighbourhood and went 'all hippy' for a few years, living almost self-sustainably.

One of his favourite methods of cooking remains the simple homemade barbecue. A basic fire and grill is the predecessor of the towering gas contraptions us urbanites tend to opt for today, and in many parts of the world still defines a barbecue. In Markus's opinion the mouth-watering, charcoal-grilled flavour of food cooked this way cannot be beaten, and I have to agree.

TIP: Stand a piece of corrugated iron securely in a semi-circle behind your larger barbeque. This will help to both shield the fire and reflect the heat.

Markus says: Two bricks, a fire and a grill equals a barbecue. Anything more is just bourgeois.

BBQ 101

There are several levels of barbecue you can create yourself — this one can be made by absolutely anyone and is still highly effective.

Ingredients:

2 bricks

wood (driftwood, pinecones, any UNTREATED wood)

1 grill (an oven rack, grill top from a roasting pan etc.)

1. On a fire-safe surface away from overhanging trees, buildings, and flammable foliage, position the bricks on their side — a foot or two away from each other.

    Markus says: Try to make sure the bricks are level — this avoids rolling sausages later on...

2. Build a small fire between the two bricks and set it alight.

3. Allow the fire to build to a good heat, then leave it to die down.

TIP: Wrap vegetables such as potatoes, kumara or yams, parsnips and carrots in tin foil and push them directly into the embers beneath the grill. Let them cook for half an hour or so before removing them with tongs. Christmas mince pies are delicious cooked this way for dessert!

4. Once the fire has reduced to hot embers, it's cooking time. Lay the grill across the bricks and add food.

5. If the heat gets too low and the cooking slows down, build the fire back up a little to keep it going.

Change it up

If you've mastered the beginner's barbecue or you think it all sounds far too easy, you can take it to the next level. The sky is the limit — you have the basic principals, now you can get as creative as you like. Here are some ideas that Markus has used:

*   Use four (or more) bricks and a piece of corrugated iron. Set the bricks on their ends and place each as a corner of a square. Balance a piece of corrugated iron on top and use in place of a grill rack.

- Use six or more bricks to balance a caste iron plate from an old gas barbecue. Clean the plate as for corrugated iron, then 'season' it by frying onions in a little oil as you would a new wok.

- Go one step further and use 12 or more bricks to create a barbeque with levels. Place two bricks at the front to create a basic barbecue with a grill rack, then build the others higher in behind. Balance a larger rack or cast iron plate across the higher level. This will be ideal for cooking fish or vegetables whilst the lower rack deals with meat options.

Out in the car with Murray

Murray Sutcliffe was lucky enough to grow up near the local dump. There, he and his group of mates would find endless treasures and get into all kinds of trouble. The boys would head off for hours on their bikes, damming streams, chopping down trees, nicking things from people's gardens and making gunpowder from available chemicals. Ahh yes. Those were the days …

To keep him out of trouble, Murray's parents encouraged him to fix broken machinery and keep the household appliances ticking along. It was something Murray had a natural fascination for. He became very skilled, and maintained his first car — a Hillman — fastidiously. He's kept his current car running beautifully for over 20 years, and is more than a little shocked when he meets young drivers who don't know how to check their cars' oil (that would be me). Murray's grandchildren love watching him tinker with cars, and he's determined to impress on them the importance of good car maintenance.

Save yourself money and embarrassment at your service station with the following basic skills.

Your manual

First things first — your car should have a manual. Hopefully you know where it is. If you got your car second-hand (or third- or fourth-hand), it may be lurking in the back of the glove box, or it may be missing. Don't panic, there's always the internet. Type the make and model of your car into Google and you'll find plenty of information. It's a good idea to get to know the overview of your particular car before embarking on any checks as all cars are slightly different — some are more 'tinkerable' than others.

Murray says: If you get access to the right information you can do any bloody thing!

Tyre pressure

Murray suggests you should check your tyre pressure every couple of weeks. If that seems a bit excessive, at least try for every time you fill up with gas. Flatish tyres wear quicker, are more dangerous (don't brake as effectively), and can mean increased petrol consumption.

Your manual will tell you the correct tyre pressure for your make of car — but if you can't find it, just ring a tyre store and ask. They'll want to know the make and model of your car so be prepared with the details (don't say 'a blue one'). They may also ask for the tyre number. You'll find this written on the side of the tyre.

Most tyres should be around 27 kPa (kilopascals). It's normal for the front tyres to need a higher pressure than the back.

At a service station, punch the required kPa number into the air machine. Unscrew the wee cap on your tyre, and connect the air machine hose. The machine will ding at you when it reaches the right pressure. That's it! It's that easy. Don't forget to put the wee cap back onto your tyre.

Murray says: Believe it or not, air is still free!

Changing a tyre

Find out where the jack and spare tyre live in your car BEFORE YOU NEED THEM! Chances are it'll be dark and raining when you do.

If you get a flattie, here's what to do:

- Park on level, solid ground with the engine off, the car in gear and the handbrake on. Think about gradient of road (i.e. are you on a hill?) as well as curvature (i.e. is the car sloping towards the gutter?) — the car needs to be as LEVEL as possible.

- Take off the hub cap. It should unscrew relatively easily, or if you have the pop-off variety, prise around the edges with a flat screwdriver until it loosens — a little like taking the lid off a coffee can.

- Loosen the nuts of the tyre slightly (about a quarter turn each) before jacking up the car. They're often very tight, and this will make it easier.

- Make sure the ground you're on is solid enough to support the jack, and put it into position. Check your car's manual for where it should go — some cars have a plate near each wheel, others have one in the middle of each side to lift the whole side of the car.

- Insert the handle on the jack, and turn or pump it to raise the wheel. There are several different types of jacks, so again, experiment with how yours works BEFORE you need to use it one stormy night.

- Undo the nuts, and remove the wheel. Don't forget to stash the nuts somewhere you'll find them again!

- Put your spare wheel on, and reverse the above procedures — lowering the jack slowly and carefully.

- Give the wheel nuts an extra tighten when the wheel is back on the ground, and replace the hub cap.

- Take the flat tyre to get fixed ASAP!

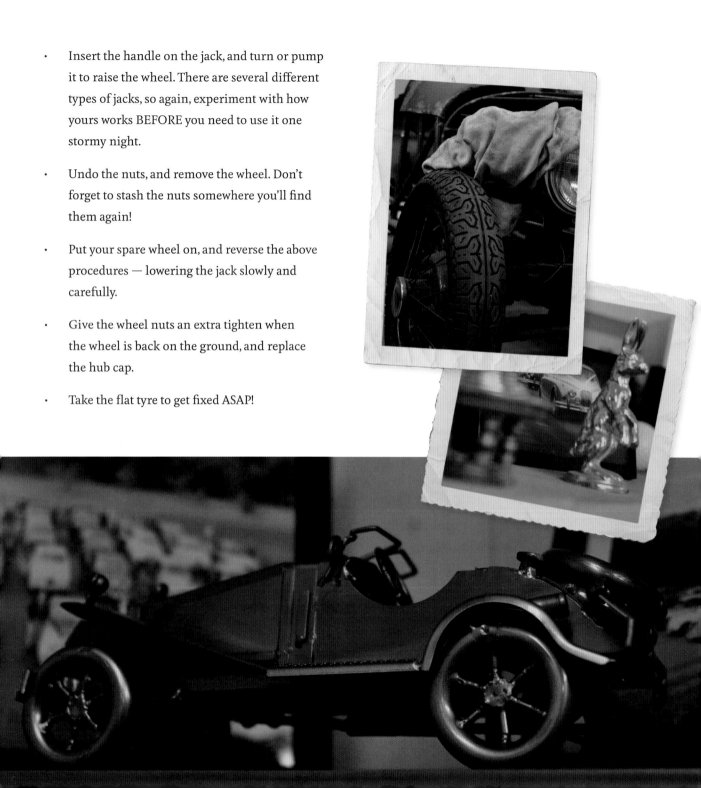

Under the hood

It may be a frightening, confusing world where you've never dared tread before — but try to get familiar with what lies beneath your car's hood. Murray recommends giving your trusty vehicle a monthly once over; checking windscreen washer, radiator, brake fluid and oil.

OPENING THE HOOD

You've probably done this before, but let's not assume anything …

- Inside the car, usually somewhere near the driver's knees, you'll find a lever which releases the hood. It may be helpfully marked 'hood', or it may have an indecipherable picture on it just to confuse you. Pull it or push it, depending on your car. You should hear a click — your hood (aka bonnet) is now unlatched.

- Feel under the hood, above the car's grill, for a safety catch. Flick it forwards or backwards until you feel the hood release.

- Once open, prop the hood open with the support rod which slots into an indent in the top corner. If it is windy, keep a hand on the hood for extra support — or get someone else to — so you don't end up squashed under the bonnet. It can happen.

Now you're in, it's time to go exploring:

Windscreen washer

Look for a plastic bottle. The one with a hose attached and a mark reading 'MAX' two-thirds of the way up is the radiator overflow bottle. You want THE OTHER ONE!!

Keep this filled up with water mixed with detergent.

Murray says: You can buy special detergent, but dishwashing liquid is as good as anything – Just put in a couple of teaspoons and top up with water.

DO NOT get your windscreen washer confused with the radiator bottle. If in doubt, swallow your pride and ask for help — yes, even if you're a guy. My friend Simon once famously released a surprise display of soap bubbles from the radiator when his car overheated on a road trip. It took a lot of flushing before the car would go again.

The radiator

The radiator overflow bottle is the plastic bottle you found before with the 'MAX' mark on it. This should be full of fluid up around the MAX mark.

If it's not, it could indicate a problem — top it up with water and book your car in for a service.

Next, take the pressure cap off the radiator. This is the metal twist cap that is usually labelled 'WARNING — Do not remove while engine is hot!' It has this label for a reason: so that you don't end up with a fountain of boiling water in your face. Only remove the cap when the engine is cool.

You should see fluid inside the radiator most of the way to the top. If it is low, top up with a 50/50 mix of water and anti-freeze. If it is regularly low, get your car seen to.

Brake fluid

This is located in a plastic reservoir, usually found towards the back of the engine. It should read 'Brake' or 'Brake Fluid'.

Never put water in here!

Open the cap, and check to make sure the fluid level is fairly high. If you check regularly you'll be able to spot if it's decreasing. If so there may be a leak, which will need to be fixed as soon as possible.

If you want to top up the brake fluid yourself, make sure you do some research on which type of fluid your car uses. This may also be marked on the brake fluid cap.

Checking the oil

First, find your dipstick.

This is a small looped handle, often yellow (but not always), usually found towards the centre of the engine. It looks a little like the end of a metal skewer. If your car is an automatic there'll be one dipstick for the engine and one for the gearbox — you want the gearbox. These should be marked.

Pull the dipstick gently and it should come out easily. Wipe the end on a paper towel or tissue, plunge it back in, then pull it out again to read it.

Towards the bottom of the dipstick you'll see two labelled marks or dots — one hot, one cold. The oil level on the stick should fall between these two extremes, never above or below.

If your oil's looking a little low, you'll need to top it up. Pop the dipstick back into place, and remove the oil filling cover. This is the big metal knob nearby marked 'Oil', 'Engine Oil' or similar.

TIP: If you're a city slicker and your car is usually used for short trips, do take it for a good run on the open road occasionally. This gives the engine a chance to get properly hot and blow off contaminants – a little like taking yourself for a good run.

Get some new oil OF THE RIGHT TYPE! If you've had your oil changed at a service station they may have left a sticker in your window with the type of oil used. Some cars' oil-filling caps will be labelled with the oil type. Otherwise, check your manual.

Pour in the oil carefully — start with just half a litre. Wait a minute or two for the oil to bog its way down to the bottom, then check the dipstick again. Repeat until your oil reaches a good level (just UNDER the higher dot/mark).

CHAPTER TWO
THE GREAT INDOORS

Painting a room with Jack

Jack Warren is koro (grandfather) to eight grandchildren, and four great-grandchildren. He's achieved a lot in his time, starting his working life as a teenage apprentice in the refrigerator trade.

A hard-working-common-sense sort of a chap, Jack set his mind on building the family a home when he got married. He took on a new apprenticeship as a builder, and by the time his children came along he had his own house to his name. The house that Jack built is still standing strong, and has become the much-loved home of his granddaughter. Jack went on to build a second house that he now lives in himself.

Though Jack is well into his retirement years, he can almost always be found up a ladder in his overalls painting or patching something. He and his life-long friend Brian still took on paid building work for people until only a few months ago, when Brian sadly passed away.

Jack is a firm believer in giving things a go, and reckons painting a room is a skill that almost anyone can master but that many inadvertently get wrong.

'It's 90 per cent common sense, 10 per cent tricks of the trade.'

Jack says: Anyone half-way decent with their hands can do it.

Prepping

I know, I know — prepping is boring. Everyone always goes on about how important it is and all you think is, 'blah blah blah, I just want to slap on some colour and have that wall looking good'. Me too. But prepping a surface before you paint it is often the difference between a good paint job and a hot mess. It doesn't need to take long, and you'll have the right to congratulate yourself every time you look at your beautiful wall ever after. That's got to be worth it . . .

Ingredients:

plastic bags

old bed sheets or drop cloths

filler/plaster (found at hardware store)

sponge

sugar soap (or simple detergent)

water

sandpaper

1. Move all your furniture out of the room if possible, or at least pile in the centre and cover it with drop cloths or old bed sheets.

2. Lay drop cloths or sheets over the floor.

3. Take down any curtains, and loosen the light fittings and electrical socket covers so that they hang a little away from the wall or ceiling. Wrap a plastic bag around each to save them from paint splotches.

4. Check your wall for any holes or gaps — such as dents in the plaster, grooves between joins, or holes where a nail once fitted.

5. Use a suitable filler or plaster to cover these gaps should you find any. Don't be intimidated — this is not hard! Your local hardware store will give you good advice on which filler is best for the job, and it will come with simple instructions.

6. When the filler is dry, use sandpaper to smooth it flush with the line of the wall.

7. Mix sugar soap or a household detergent into a bucket of water, and sponge clean the walls to get rid of any dirt or dust. The sponge should be soaked but not dripping wet. A sponge mop is ideal for reaching high, and will save you some time up a ladder.

8. When the walls are dry, use medium or fine grain sandpaper to give all the surfaces you are about to paint an all-over light sand. This step is important! It allows the paint to grip the surface properly; skipping it will only cost you time and paint later on.

Painting

Ingredients:

paint

stirrer

masking tape

brushes

roller & tray (optional)

undercoat (optional)

1. Buy the right paint! Different rooms require different types of paint. With wet areas like bathrooms and laundries this is particularly important. These days there's a wide range of options — a paint or hardware store will be able to advise you.

> TIP: Before you head to the paint store, make sure you've measured the room you're about to paint. Take note of the number of square metres, then check the label on the paint tin or ask in the paint store to see how much paint you'll need.

2. Start at the beginning. It's almost impossible to create a perfectly straight line with a paintbrush, so where you'll have two paint colours coming together or a painted surface meeting a non-painted surface, carefully lay masking tape along the borderline.

> TIP: When applying masking tape, it's a good idea to unravel the roll slowly, pressing the tape along the line of your surface as you go. Use the back of a spoon or knife to smooth it securely into place.

3. Stir your paint with a stirrer — a strong flat stick will do the trick. Make sure you stir thoroughly, scraping any residue off the bottom of the can.

> TIP: You can start with undercoat, but provided your wall is not brand new, you may want to opt for two layers of topcoat instead. Jack often chooses this approach to get the most depth from a paint colour.

4. Even if you plan to use a roller for the most part, first use a brush to paint around the edges of your wall, along the ceiling line, and any masking tape lines. A brush allows you to be far more accurate and get right into the corners and edges.

Jack says: never dip the whole brush into the paint — just the first 30mm.

Jack says: The key to painting is an even application.

TIP: A brush is really the only tool that's essential for painting, and Jack's advice is that it's definitely worth investing in a good one. A quality brush will give you much better results and, if well looked after, will offer far more value for money in the end. Jack once painted an entire house with a single 4-inch brush!

TIP: Sometimes of course it's not possible, but if you can, try to finish one whole surface (e.g. one wall, one ceiling, one windowsill) in a single session — before taking a break. This will help prevent uneven lines where one part has dried before the other.

5. A good quality roller can certainly speed up the job. Once you've gone around the edges of your wall with a brush, roll the paint onto the wall starting at the top and working down to the bottom. Use firm pressure on the roller but don't push too hard or it'll go skidding off sideways.

6. Paint your ceiling using the same techniques as for a wall, starting with a brush and — if you have one — moving on to a roller for the main section. Work from one side of the ceiling to the other in an even pattern.

7.   Now for the fiddly bits. Paint skirting boards by starting at the top of the board and working down to halfway in short strokes. Go over these strokes with long horizontal strokes to smooth them.

8.   Use a piece of cardboard to protect the floor as you move along it with the same technique, only this time working from the bottom up.

9.   Doors are best painted with a brush, not a roller, unless they are completely flat with no panelling. If possible remove door handles first, or at least wrap a plastic bag around them to stop paint drips.

10.   Open windows to paint them! Use a brush, and apply masking tape along the joins with a wall to prevent spill over. Make sure the paint is dry before closing the window or you'll seal it shut.

Painting your own interior can save you a lot of money, and will give you the satisfaction of having 'done it yourself' — even if larger DIY jobs are not your thing.

CHAPTER FOUR
DRESS UP

On a shoe string with Kevin

When Kevin was growing up during the Depression, material goods were difficult to come by. Making things last as long as possible was part of daily life. People of Kevin's generation find it hard to fathom the way we so often treat products as disposable these days, especially now that many items are made cheaply and money is more readily available. For a lot of us, though, money doesn't flow out of the wall machine quite as easily as it used to. And on top of that, we're beginning to realise that the making-then-trashing pattern can't be sustained forever.

Though Kevin claims the knowledge he has to offer 'is just plain common sense', it's valuable advice. Kevin works in a shoe repair business, a trade which he watched his father and brother-in-law enter before him. Like many of his era Kevin is from a large family, but because he was the only boy he escaped the chain of hand-me-downs relegated to his sisters. New shoes were a sought-after treasure, and Kevin learned to care for them assiduously. To this day he owns a pair of dancing shoes that he bought as a young man nearly 50 years ago, which amazingly still have their original heel and sole.

Polishing your shoes

Ingredients:

shoe cream (colour of your shoes or neutral)

shoe brush

soft cloth (or old pantyhose)

1. Wipe away any dust or dirt on the shoe using a damp cloth. Make sure the heel and sole are clean too.

2. Keeping one of your hands inside the shoe to maintain its shape, use one end of the shoe brush to apply the cream to your shoe.

3. Use the other end of the brush to give your shoe a good initial buff.

4. Finish off with a vigorous buff using the soft cloth or old pantyhose. This will bring up the shine on the shoes and have them looking like new.

Kevin's advice is to polish up shoes once a week if you wear them regularly, otherwise once a month will suffice for your 'occasion' shoes.

TIP: Choose a good quality shoe cream rather than a wax shoe polish, as it will deeply moisturise and protect the shoe leather.

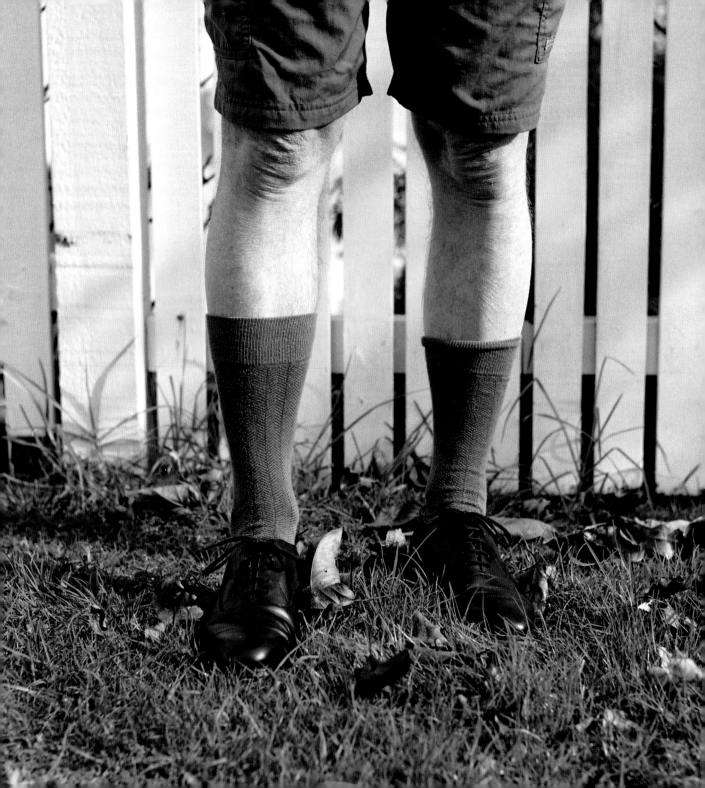

Des says: It's a nice, neat knot — very smart indeed.

Tie-ing the knot with Des and John

Des Smith and John Jolliff are two of the most generous, hospitable, and entertaining grandads you could hope to meet. Their relationship has spanned nearly quarter of a century, and the couple still live in the house that Des built himself. Des has always been passionate about gardening (see page 10), and their uniquely designed house has stunning natural light with views of the garden from every angle.

The duo has plenty of sound advice for the grandkids, two of whom arrive with freshly baked gingerbread people for Des and John as we are visiting. Of all the wisdom he can pass on to them, John believes the most valuable pearl he has learned over the years is to 'never think you're inferior or superior to anyone else'.

After years of waiting, the couple were able to legally tie the knot recently. They were — true to form — impeccably turned out on their wedding day. As a boy, Des worked Friday nights in the menswear store his older brother managed. He was paid in clothes, so he was always smartly dressed and became a deft tie-r of ties. John on the other hand claimed not to have worn a tie in 'some 20 odd years!', and is still affectionately impressed by Des's skill.

Now go paint the town red!

BOW TIE

Tying a bow tie takes a little more practice, so don't feel defeated if you don't get it right first time. Once you've mastered it, it's just like tying a shoelace — in fact, it's based on the same type of knot.

1. With your collar up, place the tie evenly around your neck, then turn your collar down over it.

Des says: Make sure your top button is done up.

> TIP: You can create a bow tie look with any tie fabric, but it'll make things easier (and neater) to use a purpose-made adjustable bow tie. These can often be found in second-hand shops. Shorten or lengthen the strap to suit your collar size before you begin.

2. Make a basic knot by passing the right side over the left, and up through the centre gap. This should sit tightly (ish — don't choke yourself!) at your throat.

3. Hold the end of the right length and fold it back on itself to form a bow loop. Pinch to hold at the centre point — in front of your buttons.

4. Pass the loose left end up through the gap and over the top of this bow loop.

5. You should notice another tighter loop has now been created at the back of the knot. Reach through the tight loop and pull the middle of the left length through. This will create the other bow loop.

6. Pull both loops to tighten, and tidy a little — pushing out any creases with your finger tips.

What are you waiting for? Get your tails on and go dazzle a crowd!

Mending a zipper

You know the moment, usually when you're running late for something important, you go to tug up the zipper of your favourite jacket/jeans/dress/super-retro track top and it just won't happen. Desperate, you wrench at it until inevitably you end up with the zip-tag halfway up the teeth and neither end of the zipper actually closed. It's a tragedy which has led to the disposal of many an item of clothing. The good news is, there's an easy fix. It won't stop you running late, but it will save your zippered clothes . . .

Ingredients:

1 needle

1 pair pliers

50 cm embroidery thread

1. Using the pair of pliers from your household toolkit (see page 45), tug at the metal stopper at the bottom of your zipper until it comes off. This can be quite tricky but it's all about brute force; give it a bit of grunt.

2. Pull the zip-tag down to the very bottom being careful to stop before it runs off the teeth.

3. Line up the teeth of the zipper so that both sides are straight without any bunching.

4. Begin to pull up the zip-tag slowly, making sure the zip teeth are locking together the way they are supposed to. If not, pull the tag down and begin again. Aim to get it about halfway up correctly.

5. Once you're confident the teeth are in place, thread your needle with a double thread (see Buttons on page 91). You are going to create stitches to replace the metal stopper.

6. Pass the needle up from the underside of the fabric in the location that one side of the metal stopper used to sit.

7. Pass the needle back down through the fabric on the opposite side of the old stopper location.

8. Continue to create these stitches, going over and over the whole area once occupied by the metal stopper.

9. When you feel you've done enough to create a proxy 'stopper', pass the needle into the underside of the fabric and create a couple of light anchor stitches before cutting the thread.

10. Zip up your zipper!

Patching

A tear or stain in good clothing doesn't have to mean the end of it. It can be a chance to get creative! Grandad's clothes were full of patches back in the day, and happily for us the decoupage look is socially acceptable again.

TIP: When finding a patch, make sure you've first measured the area of clothing you're trying to cover. It's not so useful to have half a hole gaping out from under the patch. Your patch should be larger than the area you're covering.

IRON-ON PATCHES

If you feel like you're wearing a giant baseball glove when it comes to handling a sewing needle, you'll be pleased to know the modern world has come up with a way in which you can still mend clothing. The iron-on patch is exactly as it sounds — a pre-made patch that you simply iron on to the worn or torn area of your clothing. They're usually easily available from craft stores, department stores and some supermarkets.

Iron-on patches are particularly good for kids' clothes as they are a quick fix and can come in the form of their favourite pirate/princess/singing monkey.

PATCHY PATCHES

Old school patching, where one fabric covers another, is stronger than its iron-on counterpart. You don't have to be a regular sewing fanatic for the simple hand stitching it requires, and it can be fun to play with different fabrics until you find a look you like. Some people use a more complex stitch for patching, but this one is easy to grasp and will do the job just fine.

Ingredients:

pre-made patch or other fabric

1 needle

1 pin

50 cm cotton thread

masking tape (optional)

1. Buy a pre-made patch, or select a piece of strong fabric that you think will suit the look of the clothes you're mending.

2. If using fabric, cut it to the shape and size you want in order to cover the damaged area of clothing.

3. If your clothing has a rip or hole in it, carefully turn the item inside out and tape the torn piece with a little masking tape on the underside to keep it flat.

4. Position the patch where you want it to be, and pin it lightly in place.

5. Thread the needle and knot the bottom of the thread.

6. Pass the needle up through the underside of the fabric into one edge of the patch, and pass it back down into the clothing about half a centimetre away.

7. Bring the needle back up and continue in this pattern until you've sewn around the patch. Keep the stitches as even as possible.

8. Finish with two or three stitches underneath the patch on the underside of the clothing only, then cut the thread.

You're patched and ready to go!

Darning

No more holey socks stuffed in the back of your sock drawer — resurrect them with this simple darning technique. Darning is a very effective way of mending holes in fabric, especially wool. It's almost certainly what would have held your grandparents' socks together for years!

TIP: It helps to think of darning as being more like weaving than sewing. This gives a better sense of how the stitches are supposed to work.

Ingredients:

embroidery thread (or wool if darning a wool garment)

1 large needle (ideally a darning needle)

something small & round (softball, plastic ball, an orange . . .)

1. Select a thread that matches the sock you are mending, and thread your needle. If possible you want to mend the entire hole with just one piece of thread, so make sure it's nice and long.

2. Put your round thing into the sock and position it under the hole. This takes the place of your foot in giving the sock its shape. Pull the sock taut and hold in place to keep the hole open.

3. Starting a centimetre or so from the edge of one side of the hole, weave the tip of the needle in and out of the sock's fabric.

4. When the needle extends beyond the width of the nearby hole, pull it through — stopping before the end of the thread.

5. Weave the tip of the needle back the other way again, alongside and parallel to your first stitch line.

6. Continue creating these lines, even when you reach the hole itself. Pass the thread over the hole like a bridge. Make sure the beginning of your weave stitches start far enough back from the hole to hold strong.

7. Stop when you have as many weave lines on the far side of the hole as you do on the original side. You should now be looking at a rectangle of stitches, with the hole underneath them in the centre.

8. Turn the needle 90°, and repeat the process — this time perpendicular to your first set of lines. When you reach the hole, weave the needle through the 'bridge' threads you created earlier.

9. Trim the thread leftover from your first and last stitch, and cut away any flaps of sock that are sticking out near the hole.

10. Welcome your sock back to the outside world!

Homebrew with Nev

As I write this page, Neville & Dawn Barker are out celebrating their Golden Wedding Anniversary. For much of their impressive 50 years together they've been working in the hotel trade, becoming highly popular publicans. Nowadays they have retired to the little cottage they renovated, but the sense of their former existence is kept very much alive by a home-built bar that takes up at least a quarter of their lounge, and the buckets of Nev's beer brewing in the spare bedroom.

During their time in hotels, doing things yourself was more a necessity than an option. 'If the toilet was bung you'd fix it', Nev remembers fondly. 'It was just the way of the world.' He was inspired by Dawn's father, who was a chemist by trade but could turn his hand to anything. 'He wore a suit and tie during the week, then it was boots, shorts and a shovel in the weekend.' Neville's first foray into homebrew was born from the fact that there were no bottle stores anywhere near their cottage. True to form, he simply shrugged his shoulders and began making beer himself.

Nev reckons brewing your own beer 'works out pretty cheap'; less than a quarter of the price of buying it. His homebrew certainly proves very popular with his six young-adult grandchildren, who stop by grandad's place when they're running low. Nev endeavours to retrieve the bottles when they're empty, but with somewhat limited success. He doesn't mind though, and gets a new brew going about once a month to keep up supply (depending on how many grandkids are around!). At any rate, he says, it's almost healthy. Nev's secret trick-of-the-trade is using malt instead of sugar, which he claims makes the beer practically a health tonic. He remembers his mother regularly lining him up with his six siblings and shoving a spoonful of malt extract into each of their mouths. She clearly knew something about health, because at 100 years old Nev's mother can still be found taking great striding walks down the beach.

Homebrew beer

This easy recipe for homebrew uses a supermarket brewing kit. Yes, that's right — a kit. After many years of trial and error, Nev has concluded that making beer from scratch (cooking up hops in a barrel) is too fiddly, too time-consuming, takes up far too much space and is most of all, unnecessary. These days kits are easy to come by, better quality, and are in fact less expensive than doing everything the traditional way. Nev did start out the hard way though. When he and Dawn were first married, he and his housemate used to brew hops in the washing copper. No washing could be done for a week or more while they were waiting for it to ferment. Dawn was less than impressed, and worse still Nev says, 'it tasted bloody terrible!'

Ingredients:

1 can of brewing kit (found in the beer/wine section of your supermarket)

1 kg malt (optional, or replace with sugar)

15 litres boiled tap water (cooled to room temperature)

½ cup lukewarm water

TIP: Before you start, clean and sanitise EVERYthing you're going to be working with, from pots to plastic tubing. Nev can't emphasise this enough! Wash all equipment in hot water (no soap), then use sanitising tablets from the supermarket or pharmacy to deal with any leftover would-be bugs.

Nev says: The key to successful beer is good sanitation.

1. In a large stainless steel soup pot, bring 5-7 litres of water to the boil.

2. Stir in the hopped malt extract from your brewing kit, and the additional malt. This malt replaces the sugar that is listed on the kit's instructions. It's optional, but it will give you healthier, better tasting beer!

TIP: If you live in a cold climate, first heat the tin of extract slightly by placing it into a bowl of hot water. This will make the contents easier to get out.

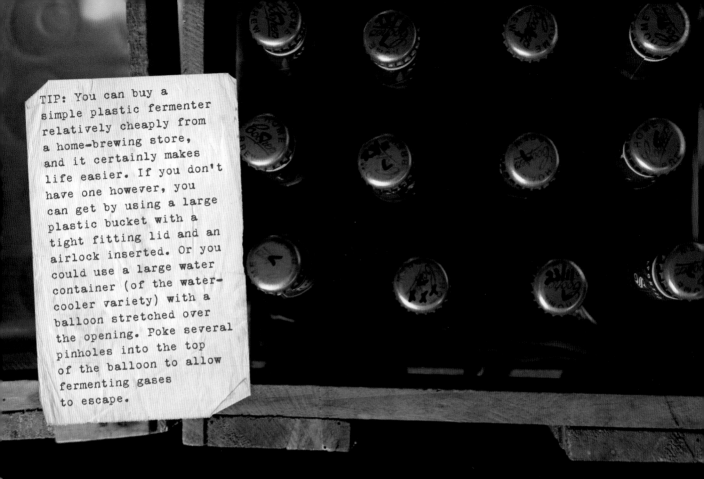

TIP: You can buy a simple plastic fermenter relatively cheaply from a home-brewing store, and it certainly makes life easier. If you don't have one however, you can get by using a large plastic bucket with a tight fitting lid and an airlock inserted. Or you could use a large water container (of the water-cooler variety) with a balloon stretched over the opening. Poke several pinholes into the top of the balloon to allow fermenting gases to escape.

3. Continue to stir until the malt has completely dissolved, then remove the pot from the heat and cover.

4. Fill your fermenter with 15 litres of cool water. If you're using tap water, it's best to boil it first to remove impurities.

5. Add the contents of your pot to the water in the fermenter, cover, and leave to cool to room temperature (if not already).

6. Pour the yeast from your kit into half-a-cup of lukewarm water (25°C). Make sure the water is not too hot! Room temperature is usually about right. This step won't be on the kit's instructions, but it gives the yeast a handy kick-start when it has been sitting in the packet for a while.

7. When you're sure your brew is cool enough, add the yeast mixture.

8. Cover your fermenter or bucket and leave the brew to ferment for a week.

Bottles

Beer can be very simply bottled in recycled, plastic, soft drink bottles with screw tops. If you prefer, use empty glass beer bottles and get yourself a capping device to put on new caps. Caps and cappers are available from brewing stores and some supermarkets. They're not expensive and, of course, beer in beer bottles feels more like the real deal. If you are a beer drinker I'm guessing bottle supply won't be a problem.

9. Put half a teaspoon of sugar into each of your sterilised bottles, and siphon in the brew. A store-bought fermenter will usually have a tap near the bottom which makes this process easy, but if you're making do with a bucket, use a length of clear plastic tubing to siphon the beer. Leave a gap between the beer and the top of the bottle!

Getting fancy

Once you've got the basics sorted and you're enjoying your foray into homebrew, here are a few little tricks you can try to play with the flavour of your beer.

- If you've chosen a dark beer brewing kit, try adding a few drops of liquorice essence for a lovely fuller flavour.

- If you're using sugar instead of additional malt, experiment with different types of sugar (raw, brown, corn) for different flavours.

- For an interesting twist, sugar can also be replaced with honey or molasses.

10. Cap the bottles or screw on the tops, and leave in a cool dark spot for a couple of months before drinking.

- Give your beer a spicy edge by adding herbal tea bags to the boiling water before pouring in the malt extract. Experiment with different types of tea.

Nev says: Be patient! A lot of beginners go wrong because they pop the caps too early.

Homemade cider

Ingredients:

1.5 kg cooking apples (the more sour the better)

5-6 litres water

1 kg sugar

3 lemons

TIP: Plastic soft drink bottles are ideal
for cider – best to avoid glass bottles as
cider can get fairly explosive! Thoroughly
clean plastic bottles first by putting
them and their screw tops through a
dishwasher cycle.

1. Cut the apples into rough chunks, put them in a plastic bag, and stick them in the freezer.

2. After a few days thaw the apples until they're soft enough to pulp in a blender.

3. Pulp them in a blender, adding a little water to soften the mix.

4. Pour the remaining water into a large plastic bucket, and add the pulp.

5. Cover, and keep for a week — stirring twice a day.

6. Strain the mixture through cheesecloth or clean cotton, and throw away the pulpy bits.

7. Pour the liquid back into the bucket, stirring in the sugar and the juice and zest of the lemons.

8. After 24 hours, the mixture should begin to fizz.

9. Strain again, this time pouring into bottles.

10. Screw the lids loosely onto the bottles, and leave for about a week.

Your cider is ready to be enjoyed after a week or so, but Nev reckons patience is a virtue with cider as well as beer. He leaves his brew to improve for a good two months before partaking.

Dawn says: hot in the bedroom!
Nev says: Perhaps in the shed
or somewhere . . .

Cool cordial

Neil Lambie is the kind of grandad who is flabbergasted at how much money people spend on things these days. Why buy it when you could easily make it or grow it yourself? Neil grew up on a farm, and never knew his mother to buy a vegetable. Like many a grandad, his experience was that if it wasn't in the garden, you didn't have it. His father taught him how to take care of the garden, and he passed these skills on to his four children — though he claims that one of them 'wouldn't know a cauliflower from a wallflower'. To preserve Lambie family peace, I won't mention which one.

Now in their 70s, Neil and his wife Sarah Jane (known as Janet) still do everything themselves. They have a productive little garden and make full use of its bounty. Jars of relish, jams, marmalades, chutneys and all sorts abound on their shelves — and don't go thinking its all Janet's domain. Neil makes himself handy in the kitchen and reckons it's sad if men don't have a go at cooking.

A favourite with the grandkids is the citrus cordial Neil and Janet make, from an old family recipe their great-great Aunt Sara McKee and great-granny Nicol perfected before them. It's quick, easy and no fuss — ideal for impatient types like me, and commonsense types like Neil who 'doesn't like turning these things into big events'.

Old-fashioned citrus cordial

Ingredients:

2 large oranges

2 large lemons

6 cups sugar

2 tbsp citric acid
(found in the baking section of your supermarket)

6 cups boiling water

TIP: For a different taste, swap either fruit for grapefruit.

Neil says: A bit of home preserving is a good thing for a man to do.

TIP: Once opened, store your bottle of cordial in the fridge to make it keep longer.

TIP: Cover your mixture with a tea-towel to stop bugs from going for a swim.

1. Cut the fruit into rough chunks and pop it into a kitchen whiz or food processor to mince it up (don't peel the fruit first!).

2. Put the minced fruit into a large bowl, and cover with the sugar.

3. Add the boiling water and stir until all the sugar has dissolved.

4. Leave it to cool.

5. Stir in the citric acid and leave the mixture to stand for 24 hours.

6. Strain into sterilised bottles, screw on the caps, and your cordial will keep for a year or more!

Just like store-bought cordial, dilute a little with water and an ice-cube or two (if you fancy) for a refreshing drink.

Bottles

Glass bottles with screw caps are best for this job. Recycled, commercial glass cordial bottles are ideal, or even screw-top wine bottles.

To sterilise the bottles simply clean them with hot soapy water, rinse, and put them on a tray in a cold oven. Turn the oven on to 110°C, and when it reaches that heat switch it off. Leave the bottles in the non-powered oven for 10 minutes. Sterilise the caps by simmering them for two minutes in a saucepan of boiling water. Make sure they're dry before using.

Hot Toddy

There's nothing more comforting in winter than a dash of homemade cordial and a spoonful honey stirred into a cup of hot water. It also an excellent home remedy for colds and flu (even man-flu).

TIP: Need another good reason to buy citric acid? Check out Grandad's sweets & sherbet on page 133.

Lovely liqueurs

There's many a grandpa fond of an evening tipple. In times gone by, liqueurs were often homemade and regarded as more medicinal than recreational.

In recent years there's been a surge of commercial brands and we pay a lot for the privilege, so it's worth knowing that many can be homemade for a fraction of the price — and an improvement in taste!

Nonno's limoncello

Limoncello is a sweet and refreshing lemon liqueur that has been passed down many an Italian generation. My friend Rosa, who is of Italian origin, remembers her Nonno (grandfather) insisting on a small glass of limoncello after every evening meal as a 'digestive'.

An excellent summer drink in particular, this liqueur is well worth the effort. Personally I find it difficult to restrict it to post-meal portions!

Ingredients:

1 bottle vodka (750 ml–1 litre)

5–10 lemons

2 cups sugar

1 ½ cups water

1. Wash the lemons, and peel off the zest — making sure you only get the yellow skin, not the white pith! The white part will give your liqueur an unpleasant bitter taste.

2. Place the lemon peel into an airtight glass jar, and add the vodka.

3. Close the jar and leave it to infuse for one week. Store the jar in a cool, dark spot away from sunlight.

4. When the week is up, pour the water into a pot and stir in the sugar until dissolved.

5. Heat gently and allow to boil, without stirring, for about five minutes.

6. Cool the syrup to room temperature then stir in the vodka and lemon zest.

7. Set the mixture aside for an hour or two, then give it a stir and strain the liquid into prepared glass bottles.

8. Put the bottled liqueur into the freezer overnight (or longer) and serve ice cold in chilled shot glasses.

TIP: Screw-top wine bottles or empty glass liqueur bottles are best for the job. Put them through a dishwasher cycle, or wash thoroughly with hot water then allow to dry in a warm oven.

Traditional amaretto

Amaretto is an Italian liqueur that dates back to the sixteenth century. Strictly speaking, amaretto was traditionally brewed by steeping apricot kernels and almonds in alcohol — but at least two generations of Rosa's family have enjoyed this more simple homemade adaptation. For Rosa's Nonno it is a winter alternative to limoncello. I like it all year round myself — its subtle almond flavour makes it an excellent addition in cocktails and in cooking. For a simple treat, drizzle a little over vanilla ice-cream.

Ingredients:

3 cups vodka

1 ½ cups water

1 ½ cups white sugar

¾ cup brown sugar

3 tbs pure almond essence (the real stuff if you can, not the flavoured imitation)

2 tsp vanilla essence

1. In a stainless steel saucepan, stir the white and brown sugar into the water until the sugar has dissolved.

2. Bring the mixture to the boil over a low heat, and simmer without stirring for five minutes.

3. Take the pan off the heat and allow the syrup to cool to room temperature.

4. Stir in the vodka and essences.

5. Pour into prepared glass bottles as per limoncello.

TIP: Homemade liqueurs make great gifts. Reuse pretty commercial liqueur bottles, or keep an eye out for decorative glass bottles at second-hand stores.

CHAPTER SIX
PASS IT ON

Certificate of Honour

Be it Known By All Members of
The International Guild of Knot Tyers
that

Roger Carter

Is hereby honoured for his efforts in furthering the aims and
activities of the Guild through his work as founder member and
President of the New Zealand Chapter of the I.G.K.T.
and for his contribution to the History of Cordage through
numerous publications including "Knotting Matters".

Signed by _B. E. Field_ — Guild President

Date - 01-01-01

Nuts about knots with Roger

The first time Roger Carter tied a knot he was seven years old. There had been an outbreak of diphtheria in his school class, and the young Roger found himself quarantined in a fever hospital for over four months. It was 1939 — the days before nurses wore teddy bears on their aprons and tacked up cheery pictures of cartoon animals on the walls. Afternoon rest periods were strictly observed, and woe betide any child who made a noise. Little ones like Roger, who might be tempted to pick up a toy or a comic (outrageous!), were strapped down to their beds. Unable to move far, young Roger began pulling a thread out of the aging face cloth he'd been allocated and 'messed about with it' till he formed a knot. He still remembers the sense of pride and satisfaction the achievement created, and thus began a lifetime passion.

Roger says: Without knots we'd all be nude.

Seventy-one years later, knots are still a major part of Roger's life. He went on to join the Royal Navy, where knot-knowledge was currency and 'fancywork' was highly regarded. He became an expert at rigging up the hammocks they slept in, and supplemented his pay cheque by making dog leads with some elaborate cord skills.

These days Roger is a card-carrying member of the International Guild of Knot Tyers (oh yes, there is one) and passes his knowledge on to the next generation. He runs classes for boaties and young would-be pirates, has published articles on knots, and has even been called as an expert witness in two murder trials. It's amazing where knots can take you . . .

We all use knots everyday — on clothes, shoes, luggage and plenty more — but 'knot' many of us (Grandad's joke), know how to tie anything more useful than the simple stuff. Here are a couple of handy ones Roger recommends to get you started on your own path to knot-love.

The Clove Hitch

This useful knot is not particularly strong, but will effectively lash one object to another. Amongst other uses it's the starting point for building a survival shelter, so it's a handy one to know in case you ever get caught out (or end up on a reality show).

1. Loop your rope around a pole or post.

2. Loop one end back around again, crossing over the first to form an X on the post.

3. Continue the loop, but as you bring the end back around, thread it under the meeting point of the X.

4. Pull to tighten.

The Drummer's Plait

This very simple knot has many names, amongst them the Chain Sennet or Monkey Braid. It was developed for the cords holding up drums in marching bands and the military, so it's a good looking knot as well as a useful one. The Drummer's Plait is mostly used nowadays to temporarily shorten ropes or cords. But a less well-known bonus function is that it's ideal for fixing broken bag straps, or even creating new ones. The nature of the chain means the weight of the bag will be distributed evenly across your shoulder — making for a quick, comfy (and attractive) repair.

1. With one hand, form a loop with the top end of the rope.

Roger says: Knots are not a dying art — they're still an essential part of life, used in over a hundred trades, professions and pastimes.

2. With the other hand, form a bend in the rope just below the loop, and pull this bend loosely through.

3. You now have a second loop.

4. Reach through the gap and pull a third loop through, then a fourth etc until you reach the bottom of the rope.

5. Pull the bottom end through the final loop to finish.

The simplest of toys with John

John Spittal is the epitome of a storybook grandad. With ever a twinkle in his eye he is fun, resourceful, and can usually be found creating new toys for the grandkids.

Not one to bah-humbug modern inventions, John is a fan of the internet and other new-fangled gadgets. But he firmly believes we shouldn't forget the simple stuff, especially when it comes to toys. In John's experience, the toy itself is only the beginning — the launch pad from which the child's imagination can run wild. The more simple the toy, the bigger the imagination.

Woodworking goes back several generations in John's family, at least as far as his great-grandfather who was a cooper. The young John was determined he'd never go into woodwork himself, but fate had other ideas and John went on to marry Jo — whose father, it turned out, was also a woodworker. Three children later, money was getting tight and John started crafting toys after work for the kids to play with. In the weekends he began making intricate salad tongs to sell. One project led to another, and by the time he became a grandfather John found himself secretary of his local woodworkers guild.

With a lifetime of skills and a passion for old-fashioned tools, John is only too keen to pass on his knowledge to the next generation. Here's a very simple idea that anyone can do, even if you've never worked with wood before.

TIP: Get as creative as you like with decorating the blocks — paint on pictures, numbers, letters or patterns. Older children will love to get involved.

Good ol' wooden blocks

No matter how old you are or where you grew up, chances are your childhood memories involve wooden blocks somewhere along the line. Yet when my own young daughter reached the build-and-bash stage a few years ago, I found them surprisingly hard to come by. After all, they're just shaped pieces of wood — does that really require an alarmingly expensive trip to the super-high-end children's store? Not if you make them yourself, says John.

Ingredients:

a saw (if you don't have one, borrow one)

a pencil

sandpaper

scraps of wood (firewood or off-cuts)

1. Find some wood scraps. This can be leftover firewood, or off-cuts from a friend or local hardware store. If you're lucky, it'll be free! Whatever you use though, make sure the wood has not been treated for building purposes as this will make it toxic. If in doubt, ask.

2. Using your saw, cut the wood down into workable sized pieces if it's not already.

3. With a pencil, draw different shapes onto your pieces of wood — triangles, squares, circles, random shapes. You can skip this step, but it sometimes helps the cutting process, especially the first time you make blocks.

4. Cut the shapes out with the saw. Relax, they don't need to be perfect! Odd shaped pieces get the imagination going. Just make sure they're a big enough size to avoid being swallowed by toddlers.

John says: You can find really good tools cheaply second-hand — look for a saw with a nicely shaped handle, and a blade made of spring steel.

John says: A coping saw will help you cut curves. They're fairly cheap and the great secret of the woodworking world!

5. Smooth the wood with a piece of sandpaper (or a hand sander if you have one). This part of the process is well worth it, because you want the blocks to feel nice to handle and not leave splinters. Concentrate on any sharp edges in particular.

6. Your blocks are ready for play! You can leave them as they are, paint them bright colours with kid-friendly paint, or protect them naturally by rubbing on linseed oil from an organics store.

If you're short on time, make a block here and there until the set builds up over time. A good set of wooden blocks can last generations.

TIP: Ordinary poster paint is recommended for kids' toys. It's easy to find, not expensive and non-toxic. Children love vibrant colours.

Games for the (grand)kids with Norman

A New Yorker by origin, Norman Kabak has always liked to figure out how things work. His father had little education, but taught himself about the world by reading the *New York Times* assiduously. As a young boy Norm, too, gained much of his knowledge from the media. His eyes were opened to the universe of basic science by a 1950s children's television programme called *Watch Mr Wizard*.

The now legendary character of Mr Wizard would conduct experiments each week in his 'laboratory' and explained what makes things work and why. It was an inspiration that remains with Norm today and — as a fulltime grandad these days — he's passing on his enthusiasm to the next generation.

No need to dig into your wallet and head to the toy store — there's plenty of great entertainment for kids in your own home already. Here are a few classic favourites that will keep the grizzles at bay for a while, and open a door into a world of wonder in the process.

TIP: We've all seen plastic bags flying
down the street or out of rubbish dumps
and across town. We know they can fly –
turning these into kites is a way to use
that capacity in a positive way!

Let's go fly a kite

Kite flying is an age-old sport that's fun no matter how old you are — and it's even better when you made the kite yourself! Kite making is not only a lesson in air movement and wind power, it's also (in this case) a great recycling exercise.

Ingredients:

1 plastic bag

2 sticks

string

ribbon, fabric or party streamers

1. Find two sticks, one slightly longer than the other. These can be twigs (if they're straight), bamboo garden stakes, or even kebab skewers. The size of your sticks will determine the size of your finished kite.

2. Place your sticks together in a 't' shape, the shorter one lying horizontally across the longer one. Tie them securely in place with some string, or use tape if you prefer.

3. Lie the sticks on top of your plastic bag (recycled supermarket bags or rubbish bags are ideal), and cut the bag in a diamond shape to fit the stick frame. The corners of the diamond should be just slightly beyond the points of the sticks.

4. Tie the corners of the plastic diamond securely to the points of the stick with string or tape. Make sure the plastic is taut across the sticks, but not so tight that it pulls or bends.

5. Tie a piece of string loosely from one side of the 't' to the other, width-wise. If you gently tug the middle of the string once it's tied, it should form a triangle with the cross-stick as its base.

6. Next, tie the free end of a ball of string to the lowest point of the kite — the bottom of the main stick.

7. Unravel the ball enough to thread it through the middle of the triangle you created at the cross-stick.

8. Without cutting the string, tie a knot at the centre-point where the main string crosses the triangle string, and continue to unravel the ball a little.

9. Finally, tie ribbons, streamers or lengths of fabric to the bottom of the kite. This not only decorates the kite, but the weight of the fabric also helps balance the kite when it's flying.

10. Find some space and a breeze, release your kite and allow the ball of string to unravel until the kite is comfortably airborne.

Paper cup telephone

This is a real old favourite from our grandparent's generation that works so well it surprises kids (and sometimes adults . . .).

Ingredients:

2 paper cups

twine or string (anywhere from 3-30 metres)

1. Poke a hole in the centre of the bottom of each of the paper cups.

2. Thread one end of the string through one of the cups, tying a knot large enough to prevent the string from slipping through.

3. Thread the other end of the string through the hole in the remaining cup, again tying a knot.

4. Hold on to one cup, and get your child (or adult friend, no one's judging) to walk away slowly with the other one until the string is pulled tight.

5. Have one person speak into their cup, while the other person holds the other cup to their ear.

You will find that you can hear each other very well, even up to 30 metres away — provided the string or twine is tight. This is because the sound waves from your voice create vibrations that travel between the cups by way of the string. It's this very simple principle which is the foundation of telephone and radio communications.

TIP: Make sure your two buckets or cans are exactly the same size, and of course always wash them out before using! Kids might also like to paint or decorate them before you thread the rope through.

Make a windsock

Kids often pay a lot of attention to the weather, and love to get involved in monitoring it. If you live in a spot that picks up a breeze now and then, a homemade windsock is an easy and interesting way to see which direction it is coming from — just like an aeroplane pilot.

Ingredients:

1 old long-sleeved shirt (preferably grown-up sized)

30-50 cm bendable wire

masking tape (or sewing thread)

an old sock (preferably kid-sized)

a small rock

1. Cut a sleeve from an old shirt at the armpit join.

2. Bend your wire into a circle that will fit the opening of the sleeve at its largest point (the armpit end). Don't attach the wire yet.

3. Place a small rock into the toe of an old sock, and knot the sock to prevent the rock from falling out.

4. Tie the sock to a length of string, and attach this string to the wire circle. This will be the bottom of your windsock — the rock should weigh it down.

5. Tie a second length of string to the top of the wire circle, opposite the rock sock.

6. Now fold the edges of the sleeve opening around the wire, and secure it tightly with tape. If you put your hand through the wire circle, it should go into the sleeve, like a tunnel.

TIP: If you want to get fancy, you can sew the sleeve into place with a needle and thread.

7. Hang your windsock from a tree branch or outdoor beam using the string attached to the top. The rock sock should be hanging below, keeping the windsock steady. It will automatically face into the wind when there's enough of a breeze.

TIP: Make sure your windsock is in a spot where it has space to spin around and point in all directions.

Flower magic

Another old-time favourite, this one never fails to amaze.

Ingredients:

1 white flower (daisies or carnations are best)

1 tsp food colouring

½ cup water

1. Pour the water into a slim clear vase or glass.

2. Stir in the food colouring.

3. Snip the end off the flower's stem with scissors, and pop it into the vase.

4. Leave it for a few hours then come back and take a look — the white flower petals will be turning the colour of the water.

As well as being fun for kids, this activity is also a great demo of how flowers draw moisture up through their stems.

TIP: Any colour food colouring will work with this experiment, though darker colours are the most dramatic. You could try using a few flowers at a time, each in a different glass with different coloured water.

Bucket stilts

Bucket stilts are so easy to make, older kids can do it by themselves. Even high-energy types will be entertained by these, and — good news for rainy days — they are low enough to be as usable indoors as out. Stilts are a great exercise in balance, and force small speedsters to slow down and concentrate for a bit (or figure out a few things about gravity!)

Ingredients:

2 used paint buckets or strong tin cans

2 lengths twine or slim rope

1. Punch a hole in each side of the first can or bucket, just above the base. A hammer and nail are the best tools for this job.

2. Cut a length of rope or twine that's long enough to extend comfortably from your child's hand to the floor when folded in half (fold the rope, not your child).

3. Thread each end of the rope through the holes you punched, and tie the ends together tightly inside the can or bucket.

4. Repeat with the second bucket.

Give it a go! Upturn the buckets and place one foot on the base of each. Use the rope as a handle to help you walk, keeping the buckets against your feet. Once you've had enough fun, give the kids a turn.

> TIP: Bucket stilts are low enough to be relatively safe, but inevitably kids will fall off them at some point. To avoid grazes it's best to try them out on grass or carpet, and stay away from slippery floors.

Grandad's sweets and sherbet

There are many things I remember fondly about my own Grandad — the old VW Kombi he drove, his lasting affection for whisky, his bottomless supply of jokes, his bright white (too short) bowling outfit and his love of rustling up a plate of toasted sandwiches then settling down to watch *MacGyver*.

But the very best thing about visiting Grandad was that he had a secret affair with sugar. If my brother and I learned anything from *MacGyver* (apart from how to escape certain death using only a paper clip), it was the art of stealth. No secret agent could match our finely honed ability to seek out the jars of sweets stashed in Grandad's cupboards. Though he was a seasoned smuggler, we were better. He might have fooled Granny, but never us. We found many a cache of candied treasure wrapped in his cardigans, hidden behind books, pushed high on shelves or tightly under chairs. And what sealed our professionalism as thieves is that we knew to only take one or two from each location in order to avoid raising suspicion. Oh yes. We were good.

Grandad did have legitimate supplies too — and what they lacked in the excitement of discovery, they made up for in novelty. Amongst my favourites was a music box house that opened its roof to reveal chocolate cigarettes. But the treat that undeniably out-treated all treats was the rare gift of a simple paper bag full of sherbet, and — jewel in the crown — a liquorice stick for dipping.

There's something inherently grandparenty about homemade sweets. They're popular, nostalgic, use uncomplicated ingredients and take very little time to make.

Traditional taffy

Ingredients:

2 cups sugar

1 cup boiling water

1 tbsp butter

colouring (optional)

flavoured essence (optional)

1. Combine all ingredients apart from colour and flavouring (if using) in a heavy-based, stainless steel saucepan, stirring until all the sugar has dissolved.

2. Without further stirring, bring the mixture to the boil over a low heat and simmer until it reaches 130°C or passes the Hard Ball test (see chart on page 140). Remove from the heat immediately.

3. If you are using colours and/or flavoured essence, mix these in once your mixture is off the heat.

4. Pour the syrup onto a greased plate or cookie sheet to cool.

5. As soon as the mixture is cool enough to handle, pick it up and stretch it (kids love this part). Pull and twist it as you like to form it into a long, fine rope-like length.

TIP: Tackle tacky taffy by working with it over a plate greased with butter or oil. Rub a little butter on your scissors when cutting the taffy to stop it from sticking.

6. Cut the 'rope' into even-sized pieces with scissors, and leave the pieces uncovered overnight to harden up.

Grandad's butterscotch

Ingredients:

500 g brown sugar (white sugar will also work)

1/2 cup water (approx)

90 g unsalted butter

¼ tsp cream of tartar (or 1 tsp white vinegar)

few drops lemon essence or vanilla essence

1. In a heavy bottomed, stainless steel saucepan combine all the ingredients apart from the essence (or lemon juice if you are using it).

2. Without stirring, boil the mixture until it reaches 140°C, or passes the Soft Crack test (see page 140).

3. Take the saucepan off the heat immediately, and stir in the flavoured essence and/or lemon juice.

4. Pour the mixture into a well-greased shallow baking tin, and leave it to cool and set.

5. Cut or break your butterscotch into pieces and store in an airtight jar to tempt your friends and relatives!

TIP: Way back in the day, our great-grandparents used 1 tsp fresh lemon juice instead of essence. Try this as a fresh alternative, or use it as well as vanilla essence for a bit of extra zing.

TIP: When beads or crystals form on the saucepan sides while boiling, push them down gently with a damp pastry brush.

TIP: If you like a sour twang, dust your
lemon drops with a little citric acid.

Old-fashioned lemon drops

With just two ingredients, lemon drops were amongst the simplest of pleasures enjoyed in our grandparents' day.

Ingredients:

1 cup white sugar (ideally caster sugar if you have it)

2-4 lemons

1. Squeeze the lemons, and slowly stir the juice into the sugar. You want just enough juice to dissolve the sugar, so you may not need all the juice, or — depending on your lemons — you may need to add a little extra.

2. In a heavy-based saucepan, stir the mixture over a low heat until all the sugar has dissolved and the liquid is clear and transparent.

3. Adjust the temperature to high, and boil the mixture rapidly without any further stirring.

4. Test the boiling mixture regularly in cold water until it passes the Hard Crack Test (see page 140) — or 155°C if you're using a sugar thermometer — then take it off the heat immediately.

5. Use a teaspoon to drip small droplets of the syrup onto a greased plate, candy moulds, or non-stick surface.

6. Leave your Lemon Drops to cool and harden, then enjoy! Store in an airtight container.

Simple sherbet

My brother and I are not identical twins, despite a magical belief in our early years that wearing matching outfits would somehow make it so. Alas we remain four years apart (and a different gender), but perhaps the duplicate knitted jumpers had some effect — we do have our twinnie moments. One of these, strangely, was with sherbet. As I was thinking about sherbet for the first time in 20-something years, by spooky coincidence it turns out my brother was doing the same thing. At opposite ends of the country we were simultaneously researching recipes — me for this book, and he for the science class he teaches.

Once we discovered this quirk of fate we combined forces, and you can make this recipe safe in the knowledge that several dozen school kids have perfected its balance of ingredients in order to create the ultimate taste.

Ingredients:

6 heaped tsp icing sugar

1 tsp baking soda

½ tsp citric acid

½ tsp tartaric acid (optional, can be replaced with extra citric acid)

TIP: Both citric and tartaric acid are usually easily available in the baking section of your nearest supermarket. If not, a pharmacy will often stock them.

1. Shake all the ingredients together until they are thoroughly mixed.

2. Divide into separate containers and become the favourite giver-of-treats!

Kids (and grown ups) love to dip sweets into their sherbet. Liquorice sticks are ideal, as are lollipops or candy sticks.

TIP: Sherbet is not just a treat, it's a
basic science lesson. The fizzy bubbles
that form on your tongue are actually
a gas created by the chemical reaction
of an alkali (baking soda) and an
acid (citric and tartaric). They need
moisture (your saliva) to kick-start
the reaction.

TIP: If storing sherbet, make sure it is
kept dry. Resealable plastic bags or small
airtight containers will do the trick.

Sugar testing chart

Working with boiled sugar takes a bit of trial and error — don't worry if you don't get it right first time. A sugar thermometer helps take the guess-work out of it, but our grandparents managed without them. This chart will guide you through the cold water test for syrup temperature.

Pour cold water into a small bowl, then dollop a teaspoon of the boiling syrup into the water. Leave it for several seconds before trying to pick the mixture up with your fingers.	
Cotton 110-115°C	When you pull the mixture apart between your thumb and forefinger, it will form a thin thread.
Squishy 115-120°C	The syrup will form a ball between your fingers that can be squished flat.
Hard Ball 120-140°C	The syrup will form a ball between your fingers that won't dent.
Soft Crack 140-150°C	The syrup will create threads in the water that snap when you bend them.
Hard Crack 150-165°C	The syrup will create threads in the water that are hard and crack easily.
Caramel 175°C	The syrup will turn a deep gold colour.
Burnt 176°C+	You've just lost your sugar! Syrup turns very quickly from caramel to burnt, and nothing you can do will reverse that — so keep a close eye on it when boiling.

Robyn Paterson

Robyn Paterson is a television writer, director and producer who enjoyed her first foray into the book world with predecessor, *Tips from your Nana*. She lives in Wellington, New Zealand, in a big old house that obliges her new-found DIY enthusiasm by constantly falling apart. She has a five-year-old who loves learning how to make things, a cat that likes to help out, a partner who just wishes there weren't so many things brewing in the shed, and a dog called Pete, who sensibly stays (almost) out of the way.

Tammy Williams

Tammy lives and works in Auckland, New Zealand. She is surrounded by a wonderful group of friends and family who support her in her learning of photography and filmmaking. This is Tammy's second book with Robyn, the first being *Tips from your Nana*.

Robyn & Tammy would like to thank: First and foremost Vic Parsons & Kylie Sutcliffe, without whom this book would not have been possible. We would also like to thank the many people who allowed us into their houses and their lives, and the many cups of tea and conversations that came of our visits. Thanks especially to the House of Goddess and of course, Barbara Larson from Longacre Press. Thanks to Sue Lewis and the team at Random House, and Sorelle Cansino for her beautiful design work. You were all a pleasure to work with and we're so grateful for your help in bringing this book to life.

Index

Also by the author & photographer

TIPS FROM YOUR NANA, 2011

For Poppy,
who makes me want to keep learning

Published in 2011 by Murdoch Books Pty Limited.
First published by Longacre Press, 30 Moray Place, Dunedin, New Zealand

Murdoch Books Australia
Pier 8/9
23 Hickson Road
Millers Point NSW 2000
Phone: +61 (0) 2 8220 2000
Fax: +61 (0) 2 8220 2558
www.murdochbooks.com.au

Text (c) Robyn Paterson
Photographs (c) Tammy Williams
The moral right of the authors have been asserted.
Design and typeset: Gary Stewart and Sorelle Cansino / Gas Project
Researchers: Kylie Sutcliffe and Victoria Parsons

National Library of Australia Cataloguing-in-Publication entry

Author: Paterson, Robyn.

Title: Tips from your grandad / Robyn Paterson.

ISBN: 9781742663579 (pbk.)

Subjects: Home economics--Handbooks, manuals, etc.
Grandfathers.

Dewey Number: 640.41

Printed in China